Student Guest Book

We're Glad You're Here!

Copyright ©2017 TEACH Services, Inc.
ISBN -13: 978-1-4796-0845-4

TEACH Services, Inc.
PUBLISHING
www.TEACHServices.com • (800) 367-1844

DATE	NAME	CLASS	COMMENTS
			Please share a thought, comment, quote, concern, shoe size, or any other important information that may be on your mind today.

DATE	NAME	CLASS	COMMENTS
			Please share a thought, comment, quote, concern, shoe size, or any other important information that may be on your mind today.

DATE	NAME	CLASS	COMMENTS
			Please share a thought, comment, quote, concern, shoe size, or any other important information that may be on your mind today.

DATE	NAME	CLASS	COMMENTS
			Please share a thought, comment, quote, concern, shoe size, or any other important information that may be on your mind today.

DATE	NAME	CLASS	COMMENTS
			Please share a thought, comment, quote, concern, shoe size, or any other important information that may be on your mind today.

DATE	NAME	CLASS	COMMENTS
			Please share a thought, comment, quote, concern, shoe size, or any other important information that may be on your mind today.

DATE	NAME	CLASS	COMMENTS
			Please share a thought, comment, quote, concern, shoe size, or any other important information that may be on your mind today.

DATE	NAME	CLASS	COMMENTS
			Please share a thought, comment, quote, concern, shoe size, or any other important information that may be on your mind today.

DATE   NAME   CLASS   COMMENTS
Please share a thought, comment, quote, concern, shoe size,
or any other important information that may be on your mind today.

DATE   NAME   CLASS   COMMENTS

Please share a thought, comment, quote, concern, shoe size, or any other important information that may be on your mind today.

DATE	NAME	CLASS	COMMENTS
			Please share a thought, comment, quote, concern, shoe size, or any other important information that may be on your mind today.

DATE   NAME   CLASS   COMMENTS

Please share a thought, comment, quote, concern, shoe size,
or any other important information that may be on your mind today.

DATE	NAME	CLASS	COMMENTS
			Please share a thought, comment, quote, concern, shoe size, or any other important information that may be on your mind today.

DATE
NAME
CLASS
COMMENTS

Please share a thought, comment, quote, concern, shoe size,
or any other important information that may be on your mind today.

DATE	NAME	CLASS	COMMENTS
			Please share a thought, comment, quote, concern, shoe size, or any other important information that may be on your mind today.

DATE NAME CLASS COMMENTS
Please share a thought, comment, quote, concern, shoe size,
or any other important information that may be on your mind today.

DATE

NAME

CLASS

COMMENTS
Please share a thought, comment, quote, concern, shoe size,
or any other important information that may be on your mind today.

DATE   NAME   CLASS   COMMENTS
Please share a thought, comment, quote, concern, shoe size,
or any other important information that may be on your mind today.

DATE	NAME	CLASS	COMMENTS
			Please share a thought, comment, quote, concern, shoe size, or any other important information that may be on your mind today.

DATE

NAME

CLASS

COMMENTS
Please share a thought, comment, quote, concern, shoe size,
or any other important information that may be on your mind today.

DATE   NAME   CLASS   COMMENTS

Please share a thought, comment, quote, concern, shoe size, or any other important information that may be on your mind today.

DATE	NAME	CLASS	COMMENTS
			Please share a thought, comment, quote, concern, shoe size, or any other important information that may be on your mind today.

DATE	NAME	CLASS	COMMENTS
			Please share a thought, comment, quote, concern, shoe size, or any other important information that may be on your mind today.

DATE   NAME   CLASS   COMMENTS

Please share a thought, comment, quote, concern, shoe size,
or any other important information that may be on your mind today.

DATE	NAME	CLASS	COMMENTS
			Please share a thought, comment, quote, concern, shoe size, or any other important information that may be on your mind today.

DATE	NAME	CLASS	COMMENTS
			Please share a thought, comment, quote, concern, shoe size, or any other important information that may be on your mind today.

DATE	NAME	CLASS	COMMENTS
			Please share a thought, comment, quote, concern, shoe size, or any other important information that may be on your mind today.

DATE

NAME

CLASS

COMMENTS
Please share a thought, comment, quote, concern, shoe size,
or any other important information that may be on your mind today.

DATE

NAME

CLASS

COMMENTS
Please share a thought, comment, quote, concern, shoe size,
or any other important information that may be on your mind today.

DATE	NAME	CLASS	COMMENTS
			Please share a thought, comment, quote, concern, shoe size, or any other important information that may be on your mind today.

DATE	NAME	CLASS	COMMENTS
			Please share a thought, comment, quote, concern, shoe size, or any other important information that may be on your mind today.

DATE

NAME

CLASS

COMMENTS

Please share a thought, comment, quote, concern, shoe size,
or any other important information that may be on your mind today.

DATE	NAME	CLASS	COMMENTS
			Please share a thought, comment, quote, concern, shoe size, or any other important information that may be on your mind today.

DATE NAME CLASS COMMENTS

Please share a thought, comment, quote, concern, shoe size, or any other important information that may be on your mind today.

DATE	NAME	CLASS	COMMENTS
			Please share a thought, comment, quote, concern, shoe size, or any other important information that may be on your mind today.

DATE   NAME   CLASS   COMMENTS

Please share a thought, comment, quote, concern, shoe size,
or any other important information that may be on your mind today.

DATE

NAME

CLASS

COMMENTS
Please share a thought, comment, quote, concern, shoe size,
or any other important information that may be on your mind today.

DATE	NAME	CLASS	COMMENTS
			Please share a thought, comment, quote, concern, shoe size, or any other important information that may be on your mind today.

DATE	NAME	CLASS	COMMENTS

DATE	NAME	CLASS	COMMENTS
			Please share a thought, comment, quote, concern, shoe size, or any other important information that may be on your mind today.

DATE

NAME

CLASS

COMMENTS
Please share a thought, comment, quote, concern, shoe size,
or any other important information that may be on your mind today.

DATE   NAME   CLASS   COMMENTS
Please share a thought, comment, quote, concern, shoe size,
or any other important information that may be on your mind today.

DATE	NAME	CLASS	COMMENTS
			Please share a thought, comment, quote, concern, shoe size, or any other important information that may be on your mind today.

DATE	NAME	CLASS	COMMENTS
			Please share a thought, comment, quote, concern, shoe size, or any other important information that may be on your mind today.

DATE	NAME	CLASS	COMMENTS
			Please share a thought, comment, quote, concern, shoe size, or any other important information that may be on your mind today.

DATE
NAME
CLASS
COMMENTS
Please share a thought, comment, quote, concern, shoe size, or any other important information that may be on your mind today.

DATE	NAME	CLASS	COMMENTS
			Please share a thought, comment, quote, concern, shoe size, or any other important information that may be on your mind today.

DATE	NAME	CLASS	COMMENTS

DATE	NAME	CLASS	COMMENTS
			Please share a thought, comment, quote, concern, shoe size, or any other important information that may be on your mind today.

DATE

NAME

CLASS

COMMENTS

Please share a thought, comment, quote, concern, shoe size, or any other important information that may be on your mind today.

DATE   NAME   CLASS   COMMENTS

Please share a thought, comment, quote, concern, shoe size,
or any other important information that may be on your mind today.

DATE   NAME   CLASS   COMMENTS

Please share a thought, comment, quote, concern, shoe size,
or any other important information that may be on your mind today.

DATE	NAME	CLASS	COMMENTS
			Please share a thought, comment, quote, concern, shoe size, or any other important information that may be on your mind today.

DATE

NAME

CLASS

COMMENTS
Please share a thought, comment, quote, concern, shoe size, or any other important information that may be on your mind today.

DATE	NAME	CLASS	COMMENTS
			Please share a thought, comment, quote, concern, shoe size, or any other important information that may be on your mind today.

DATE	NAME	CLASS	COMMENTS
			Please share a thought, comment, quote, concern, shoe size, or any other important information that may be on your mind today.

DATE	NAME	CLASS	COMMENTS
			Please share a thought, comment, quote, concern, shoe size, or any other important information that may be on your mind today.

DATE

NAME

CLASS

COMMENTS
Please share a thought, comment, quote, concern, shoe size, or any other important information that may be on your mind today.

DATE	NAME	CLASS	COMMENTS
			Please share a thought, comment, quote, concern, shoe size, or any other important information that may be on your mind today.

DATE	NAME	CLASS	COMMENTS
			Please share a thought, comment, quote, concern, shoe size, or any other important information that may be on your mind today.

DATE   NAME   CLASS   COMMENTS

Please share a thought, comment, quote, concern, shoe size, or any other important information that may be on your mind today.

DATE

NAME

CLASS

COMMENTS

Please share a thought, comment, quote, concern, shoe size,
or any other important information that may be on your mind today.

DATE	NAME	CLASS	COMMENTS
			Please share a thought, comment, quote, concern, shoe size, or any other important information that may be on your mind today.

DATE

NAME

CLASS

COMMENTS

Please share a thought, comment, quote, concern, shoe size,
or any other important information that may be on your mind today.

DATE	NAME	CLASS	COMMENTS
			Please share a thought, comment, quote, concern, shoe size, or any other important information that may be on your mind today.

DATE	NAME	CLASS	COMMENTS
			Please share a thought, comment, quote, concern, shoe size, or any other important information that may be on your mind today.

DATE

NAME

CLASS

COMMENTS
Please share a thought, comment, quote, concern, shoe size,
or any other important information that may be on your mind today.

DATE

NAME

CLASS

COMMENTS

Please share a thought, comment, quote, concern, shoe size, or any other important information that may be on your mind today.

DATE	NAME	CLASS	COMMENTS
			Please share a thought, comment, quote, concern, shoe size, or any other important information that may be on your mind today.

DATE

NAME

CLASS

COMMENTS

Please share a thought, comment, quote, concern, shoe size,
or any other important information that may be on your mind today.

DATE

NAME

CLASS

COMMENTS
Please share a thought, comment, quote, concern, shoe size,
or any other important information that may be on your mind today.

DATE	NAME	CLASS	COMMENTS
			Please share a thought, comment, quote, concern, shoe size, or any other important information that may be on your mind today.

DATE	NAME	CLASS	COMMENTS

DATE	NAME	CLASS	COMMENTS
			Please share a thought, comment, quote, concern, shoe size, or any other important information that may be on your mind today.

DATE	NAME	CLASS	COMMENTS
			Please share a thought, comment, quote, concern, shoe size, or any other important information that may be on your mind today.

DATE	NAME	CLASS	COMMENTS
			Please share a thought, comment, quote, concern, shoe size, or any other important information that may be on your mind today.

DATE   NAME   CLASS   COMMENTS

Please share a thought, comment, quote, concern, shoe size,
or any other important information that may be on your mind today.

DATE	NAME	CLASS	COMMENTS
			Please share a thought, comment, quote, concern, shoe size, or any other important information that may be on your mind today.

DATE

NAME

CLASS

COMMENTS
Please share a thought, comment, quote, concern, shoe size, or any other important information that may be on your mind today.

DATE	NAME	CLASS	COMMENTS
			Please share a thought, comment, quote, concern, shoe size, or any other important information that may be on your mind today.

DATE

NAME

CLASS

COMMENTS
Please share a thought, comment, quote, concern, shoe size, or any other important information that may be on your mind today.

DATE   NAME   CLASS   COMMENTS
Please share a thought, comment, quote, concern, shoe size,
or any other important information that may be on your mind today.

DATE NAME CLASS COMMENTS

Please share a thought, comment, quote, concern, shoe size, or any other important information that may be on your mind today.

DATE   NAME   CLASS   COMMENTS

Please share a thought, comment, quote, concern, shoe size,
or any other important information that may be on your mind today.

DATE   NAME   CLASS   COMMENTS

Please share a thought, comment, quote, concern, shoe size, or any other important information that may be on your mind today.

DATE   NAME   CLASS   COMMENTS

Please share a thought, comment, quote, concern, shoe size,
or any other important information that may be on your mind today.

DATE	NAME	CLASS	COMMENTS
			Please share a thought, comment, quote, concern, shoe size, or any other important information that may be on your mind today.

DATE	NAME	CLASS	COMMENTS
			Please share a thought, comment, quote, concern, shoe size, or any other important information that may be on your mind today.

DATE	NAME	CLASS	COMMENTS
			Please share a thought, comment, quote, concern, shoe size, or any other important information that may be on your mind today.

DATE	NAME	CLASS	COMMENTS
			Please share a thought, comment, quote, concern, shoe size, or any other important information that may be on your mind today.

DATE	NAME	CLASS	COMMENTS
			Please share a thought, comment, quote, concern, shoe size, or any other important information that may be on your mind today.

DATE   NAME   CLASS   COMMENTS
Please share a thought, comment, quote, concern, shoe size,
or any other important information that may be on your mind today.

DATE NAME CLASS COMMENTS
Please share a thought, comment, quote, concern, shoe size,
or any other important information that may be on your mind today.

DATE	NAME	CLASS	COMMENTS
			Please share a thought, comment, quote, concern, shoe size, or any other important information that may be on your mind today.

DATE	NAME	CLASS	COMMENTS
			Please share a thought, comment, quote, concern, shoe size, or any other important information that may be on your mind today.

DATE   NAME   CLASS   COMMENTS
                                                            Please share a thought, comment, quote, concern, shoe size,
                                                            or any other important information that may be on your mind today.

DATE

NAME

CLASS

COMMENTS
Please share a thought, comment, quote, concern, shoe size,
or any other important information that may be on your mind today.

DATE	NAME	CLASS	COMMENTS
			Please share a thought, comment, quote, concern, shoe size, or any other important information that may be on your mind today.
DATE	NAME	CLASS	COMMENTS

DATE

NAME

CLASS

COMMENTS
Please share a thought, comment, quote, concern, shoe size,
or any other important information that may be on your mind today.

DATE   NAME   CLASS   COMMENTS
Please share a thought, comment, quote, concern, shoe size,
or any other important information that may be on your mind today.

DATE   NAME   CLASS   COMMENTS

Please share a thought, comment, quote, concern, shoe size, or any other important information that may be on your mind today.

DATE

NAME

CLASS

COMMENTS
Please share a thought, comment, quote, concern, shoe size,
or any other important information that may be on your mind today.

DATE   NAME   CLASS   COMMENTS

Please share a thought, comment, quote, concern, shoe size,
or any other important information that may be on your mind today.

DATE   NAME   CLASS   COMMENTS

Please share a thought, comment, quote, concern, shoe size, or any other important information that may be on your mind today.

DATE

NAME

CLASS

COMMENTS

Please share a thought, comment, quote, concern, shoe size,
or any other important information that may be on your mind today.

DATE

NAME

CLASS

COMMENTS

Please share a thought, comment, quote, concern, shoe size, or any other important information that may be on your mind today.

DATE	NAME	CLASS	COMMENTS
			Please share a thought, comment, quote, concern, shoe size, or any other important information that may be on your mind today.

DATE   NAME   CLASS   COMMENTS

Please share a thought, comment, quote, concern, shoe size,
or any other important information that may be on your mind today.

DATE   NAME   CLASS   COMMENTS

DATE	NAME	CLASS	COMMENTS
			Please share a thought, comment, quote, concern, shoe size, or any other important information that may be on your mind today.

DATE	NAME	CLASS	COMMENTS
			Please share a thought, comment, quote, concern, shoe size, or any other important information that may be on your mind today.

DATE

NAME

CLASS

COMMENTS
Please share a thought, comment, quote, concern, shoe size,
or any other important information that may be on your mind today.

DATE   NAME   CLASS   COMMENTS
Please share a thought, comment, quote, concern, shoe size,
or any other important information that may be on your mind today.

DATE	NAME	CLASS	COMMENTS
			Please share a thought, comment, quote, concern, shoe size, or any other important information that may be on your mind today.

DATE   NAME   CLASS   COMMENTS

Please share a thought, comment, quote, concern, shoe size, or any other important information that may be on your mind today.

DATE	NAME	CLASS	COMMENTS
			Please share a thought, comment, quote, concern, shoe size, or any other important information that may be on your mind today.

DATE   NAME   CLASS   COMMENTS

Please share a thought, comment, quote, concern, shoe size, or any other important information that may be on your mind today.

DATE	NAME	CLASS	COMMENTS
			Please share a thought, comment, quote, concern, shoe size, or any other important information that may be on your mind today.

DATE

NAME

CLASS

COMMENTS
Please share a thought, comment, quote, concern, shoe size,
or any other important information that may be on your mind today.

DATE	NAME	CLASS	COMMENTS
			Please share a thought, comment, quote, concern, shoe size, or any other important information that may be on your mind today.

DATE	NAME	CLASS	COMMENTS
			Please share a thought, comment, quote, concern, shoe size, or any other important information that may be on your mind today.

DATE	NAME	CLASS	COMMENTS
			Please share a thought, comment, quote, concern, shoe size, or any other important information that may be on your mind today.

DATE

NAME

CLASS

COMMENTS

Please share a thought, comment, quote, concern, shoe size,
or any other important information that may be on your mind today.

DATE	NAME	CLASS	COMMENTS
			Please share a thought, comment, quote, concern, shoe size, or any other important information that may be on your mind today.

DATE	NAME	CLASS	COMMENTS

Please share a thought, comment, quote, concern, shoe size, or any other important information that may be on your mind today.

DATE

NAME

CLASS

COMMENTS

Please share a thought, comment, quote, concern, shoe size,
or any other important information that may be on your mind today.

DATE	NAME	CLASS	COMMENTS
			Please share a thought, comment, quote, concern, shoe size, or any other important information that may be on your mind today.

DATE	NAME	CLASS	COMMENTS
			Please share a thought, comment, quote, concern, shoe size, or any other important information that may be on your mind today.

DATE   # NAME   # CLASS   # COMMENTS

Please share a thought, comment, quote, concern, shoe size,
or any other important information that may be on your mind today.

DATE	NAME	CLASS	COMMENTS
			Please share a thought, comment, quote, concern, shoe size, or any other important information that may be on your mind today.

DATE   NAME   CLASS   COMMENTS
Please share a thought, comment, quote, concern, shoe size,
or any other important information that may be on your mind today.

DATE   NAME   CLASS   COMMENTS

Please share a thought, comment, quote, concern, shoe size,
or any other important information that may be on your mind today.

DATE	NAME	CLASS	COMMENTS
			Please share a thought, comment, quote, concern, shoe size, or any other important information that may be on your mind today.

DATE　　　　NAME　　　　CLASS　　　　COMMENTS

Please share a thought, comment, quote, concern, shoe size,
or any other important information that may be on your mind today.

DATE

NAME

CLASS

COMMENTS

Please share a thought, comment, quote, concern, shoe size, or any other important information that may be on your mind today.

DATE	NAME	CLASS	COMMENTS
			Please share a thought, comment, quote, concern, shoe size, or any other important information that may be on your mind today.

DATE   NAME   CLASS   COMMENTS

Please share a thought, comment, quote, concern, shoe size,
or any other important information that may be on your mind today.

DATE	NAME	CLASS	COMMENTS
			Please share a thought, comment, quote, concern, shoe size, or any other important information that may be on your mind today.

DATE	NAME	CLASS	COMMENTS
			Please share a thought, comment, quote, concern, shoe size, or any other important information that may be on your mind today.

DATE	NAME	CLASS	COMMENTS
			Please share a thought, comment, quote, concern, shoe size, or any other important information that may be on your mind today.

DATE

NAME

CLASS

COMMENTS

Please share a thought, comment, quote, concern, shoe size, or any other important information that may be on your mind today.

DATE

NAME

CLASS

COMMENTS

Please share a thought, comment, quote, concern, shoe size, or any other important information that may be on your mind today.

DATE	NAME	CLASS	COMMENTS
			Please share a thought, comment, quote, concern, shoe size, or any other important information that may be on your mind today.

DATE	NAME	CLASS	COMMENTS
			Please share a thought, comment, quote, concern, shoe size, or any other important information that may be on your mind today.

DATE

NAME

CLASS

COMMENTS
Please share a thought, comment, quote, concern, shoe size, or any other important information that may be on your mind today.

DATE	NAME	CLASS	COMMENTS
			Please share a thought, comment, quote, concern, shoe size, or any other important information that may be on your mind today.

DATE	NAME	CLASS	COMMENTS
			Please share a thought, comment, quote, concern, shoe size, or any other important information that may be on your mind today.

DATE	NAME	CLASS	COMMENTS
			Please share a thought, comment, quote, concern, shoe size, or any other important information that may be on your mind today.

DATE

NAME

CLASS

COMMENTS
Please share a thought, comment, quote, concern, shoe size, or any other important information that may be on your mind today.

DATE	NAME	CLASS	COMMENTS
			Please share a thought, comment, quote, concern, shoe size, or any other important information that may be on your mind today.

DATE

NAME

CLASS

COMMENTS
Please share a thought, comment, quote, concern, shoe size,
or any other important information that may be on your mind today.

DATE	NAME	CLASS	COMMENTS
			Please share a thought, comment, quote, concern, shoe size, or any other important information that may be on your mind today.

DATE   NAME   CLASS   COMMENTS

Please share a thought, comment, quote, concern, shoe size,
or any other important information that may be on your mind today.

DATE

NAME

CLASS

COMMENTS

Please share a thought, comment, quote, concern, shoe size, or any other important information that may be on your mind today.

DATE	NAME	CLASS	COMMENTS
			Please share a thought, comment, quote, concern, shoe size, or any other important information that may be on your mind today.

DATE   NAME   CLASS   COMMENTS
Please share a thought, comment, quote, concern, shoe size,
or any other important information that may be on your mind today.

DATE   NAME   CLASS   COMMENTS

Please share a thought, comment, quote, concern, shoe size, or any other important information that may be on your mind today.

DATE	NAME	CLASS	COMMENTS
			Please share a thought, comment, quote, concern, shoe size, or any other important information that may be on your mind today.

DATE	NAME	CLASS	COMMENTS

DATE   NAME   CLASS   COMMENTS
Please share a thought, comment, quote, concern, shoe size,
or any other important information that may be on your mind today.

DATE   NAME   CLASS   COMMENTS

Please share a thought, comment, quote, concern, shoe size,
or any other important information that may be on your mind today.

DATE NAME CLASS COMMENTS

Please share a thought, comment, quote, concern, shoe size, or any other important information that may be on your mind today.

DATE	NAME	CLASS	COMMENTS
			Please share a thought, comment, quote, concern, shoe size, or any other important information that may be on your mind today.

DATE

NAME

CLASS

COMMENTS
Please share a thought, comment, quote, concern, shoe size, or any other important information that may be on your mind today.

DATE   NAME   CLASS   COMMENTS
                                                            Please share a thought, comment, quote, concern, shoe size,
                                                            or any other important information that may be on your mind today.

DATE   NAME   CLASS   COMMENTS
Please share a thought, comment, quote, concern, shoe size,
or any other important information that may be on your mind today.

DATE   NAME   CLASS   COMMENTS

Please share a thought, comment, quote, concern, shoe size,
or any other important information that may be on your mind today.

DATE	NAME	CLASS	COMMENTS
			Please share a thought, comment, quote, concern, shoe size, or any other important information that may be on your mind today.

DATE	NAME	CLASS	COMMENTS
			Please share a thought, comment, quote, concern, shoe size, or any other important information that may be on your mind today.

DATE   NAME   CLASS   COMMENTS
Please share a thought, comment, quote, concern, shoe size,
or any other important information that may be on your mind today.

DATE NAME CLASS COMMENTS
Please share a thought, comment, quote, concern, shoe size,
or any other important information that may be on your mind today.

DATE

NAME

CLASS

COMMENTS

Please share a thought, comment, quote, concern, shoe size, or any other important information that may be on your mind today.

DATE   NAME   CLASS   COMMENTS

Please share a thought, comment, quote, concern, shoe size, or any other important information that may be on your mind today.

DATE   NAME   CLASS   COMMENTS
Please share a thought, comment, quote, concern, shoe size,
or any other important information that may be on your mind today.

DATE

NAME

CLASS

COMMENTS

Please share a thought, comment, quote, concern, shoe size,
or any other important information that may be on your mind today.

DATE	NAME	CLASS	COMMENTS
			Please share a thought, comment, quote, concern, shoe size, or any other important information that may be on your mind today.

DATE	NAME	CLASS	COMMENTS
			Please share a thought, comment, quote, concern, shoe size, or any other important information that may be on your mind today.

DATE	NAME	CLASS	COMMENTS

DATE   NAME   CLASS   COMMENTS

Please share a thought, comment, quote, concern, shoe size,
or any other important information that may be on your mind today.

DATE	NAME	CLASS	COMMENTS
			Please share a thought, comment, quote, concern, shoe size, or any other important information that may be on your mind today.

DATE	NAME	CLASS	COMMENTS

Please share a thought, comment, quote, concern, shoe size, or any other important information that may be on your mind today.

DATE

NAME

CLASS

COMMENTS
Please share a thought, comment, quote, concern, shoe size,
or any other important information that may be on your mind today.

DATE	NAME	CLASS	COMMENTS
			Please share a thought, comment, quote, concern, shoe size, or any other important information that may be on your mind today.

DATE	NAME	CLASS	COMMENTS
			Please share a thought, comment, quote, concern, shoe size, or any other important information that may be on your mind today.
DATE	NAME	CLASS	COMMENTS

DATE   NAME   CLASS   COMMENTS
                                                            Please share a thought, comment, quote, concern, shoe size,
                                                            or any other important information that may be on your mind today.

DATE   NAME   CLASS   COMMENTS

Please share a thought, comment, quote, concern, shoe size,
or any other important information that may be on your mind today.

DATE   NAME   CLASS   COMMENTS

Please share a thought, comment, quote, concern, shoe size, or any other important information that may be on your mind today.

DATE   NAME   CLASS   COMMENTS
Please share a thought, comment, quote, concern, shoe size,
or any other important information that may be on your mind today.

Please share a thought, comment, quote, concern, shoe size,
or any other important information that may be on your mind today.

DATE

NAME

CLASS

COMMENTS
Please share a thought, comment, quote, concern, shoe size,
or any other important information that may be on your mind today.

DATE	NAME	CLASS	COMMENTS
			Please share a thought, comment, quote, concern, shoe size, or any other important information that may be on your mind today.

DATE   NAME   CLASS   COMMENTS

Please share a thought, comment, quote, concern, shoe size, or any other important information that may be on your mind today.

DATE	NAME	CLASS	COMMENTS
			Please share a thought, comment, quote, concern, shoe size, or any other important information that may be on your mind today.

DATE	NAME	CLASS	COMMENTS
			Please share a thought, comment, quote, concern, shoe size, or any other important information that may be on your mind today.

DATE   NAME   CLASS   COMMENTS
Please share a thought, comment, quote, concern, shoe size,
or any other important information that may be on your mind today.

DATE	NAME	CLASS	COMMENTS
			Please share a thought, comment, quote, concern, shoe size, or any other important information that may be on your mind today.

DATE NAME CLASS COMMENTS

Please share a thought, comment, quote, concern, shoe size,
or any other important information that may be on your mind today.

DATE	NAME	CLASS	COMMENTS
			Please share a thought, comment, quote, concern, shoe size, or any other important information that may be on your mind today.

DATE   NAME   CLASS   COMMENTS

Please share a thought, comment, quote, concern, shoe size, or any other important information that may be on your mind today.

DATE NAME CLASS COMMENTS

Please share a thought, comment, quote, concern, shoe size,
or any other important information that may be on your mind today.

DATE	NAME	CLASS	COMMENTS
			Please share a thought, comment, quote, concern, shoe size, or any other important information that may be on your mind today.

DATE	NAME	CLASS	COMMENTS
			Please share a thought, comment, quote, concern, shoe size, or any other important information that may be on your mind today.

DATE	NAME	CLASS	COMMENTS
			Please share a thought, comment, quote, concern, shoe size, or any other important information that may be on your mind today.

DATE	NAME	CLASS	COMMENTS

DATE

NAME

CLASS

COMMENTS
Please share a thought, comment, quote, concern, shoe size, or any other important information that may be on your mind today.

DATE   NAME   CLASS   COMMENTS
Please share a thought, comment, quote, concern, shoe size,
or any other important information that may be on your mind today.

DATE   NAME   CLASS   COMMENTS

Please share a thought, comment, quote, concern, shoe size,
or any other important information that may be on your mind today.

DATE

NAME

CLASS

COMMENTS

Please share a thought, comment, quote, concern, shoe size,
or any other important information that may be on your mind today.

DATE

NAME

CLASS

COMMENTS
Please share a thought, comment, quote, concern, shoe size, or any other important information that may be on your mind today.

www.ingramcontent.com/pod-product-compliance
Lightning Source LLC
Chambersburg PA
CBHW061232150426

42812CB00054BA/2568